SWOON

ESSENTIAL POETS SERIES 272

Guernica Editions Inc. acknowledges the support
of the Canada Council for the Arts and the Ontario Arts Council.
The Ontario Arts Council is an agency of the Government of Ontario.
We acknowledge the financial support of the Government of Canada.

/WOON

Elana Wolff

GUERNICA
EDITIONS
TORONTO • CHICAGO • BUFFALO • LANCASTER (U.K.)
2020

Michael Mirolla, editor
Cover and interior design: Rafael Chimicatti
Cover image: Elana Wolff
Guernica Editions Inc.
287 Templemead Drive, Hamilton (ON), Canada L8W 2W4
2250 Military Road, Tonawanda, N.Y. 14150-6000 U.S.A.
www.guernicaeditions.com

Distributors:
Independent Publishers Group (IPG)
600 North Pulaski Road, Chicago IL 60624
University of Toronto Press Distribution,
5201 Dufferin Street, Toronto (ON), Canada M3H 5T8
Gazelle Book Services, White Cross Mills
High Town, Lancaster LA1 4XS U.K.

First edition.
Printed in Canada.

Legal Deposit – First Quarter
Library of Congress Catalog Card Number: 2019947083
Library and Archives Canada Cataloguing in Publication
Title: Swoon / Elana Wolff.
Names: Wolff, Elana, author.
Series: Essential poets ; 272.
Description: Series statement: Essential poets series ; 272 | Poems.
Identifiers: Canadiana 20190156848 | ISBN 9781771835077 (softcover)
Classification: LCC PS8595.O5924 S96 2020 | DDC C811/.6—dc23

To Menachem,
Adi, and Odette

Contents

"וַתִּשָּׂא רִבְקָה אֶת-עֵינֶיהָ, וַתֵּרֶא אֶת-יִצְחָק; וַתִּפֹּל, מֵעַל הַגָּמָל."
"When Rebecca looked up and saw Isaac, she almost fell
from the camel."

> — Genesis 24:64, *The Living Torah*,
> translation by Rabbi Aryeh Kaplan

"But slowly, as one in swoon / To whom life creeps back …
slowly by degrees, I woke up, rose up …"

> — Elizabeth Barrett Browning, *Aurora Leigh*

"I would die of delight, or at least hit the floor in a swoon,
if ever such a transformation occurred …"

> — Robert Walser, *The Walk*, translation by
> Susan Bernofsky and Christopher Middleton

"… swooning counts as believing."

> — Franz Kafka, *Letters to Milena*,
> translation by Philip Boehm

The Months of Flooding

More rain fell than could drain. Rain filled up the riverbed

and people brought their vessels out

to ride the waters
      coursing like a mom in trouble,

south.
Rain came through the cumulus

like mantic movie music, amplified by being from the hub.

Lord, we used this very word, and heard it used by others.

Lord, the inundation and the floods.

Rain came down, the river rose.

People brought their vessels out and coursed the waters

teeming like a very troubled mom — holding to the hull and gunnels,
              head below the bow —

at odds with sun, the promise and the covenant: of what?

Pigeons wheeled (against their way) and gulls,
             the occasional raven.

She'll hold a little son to her chest,

both will sweetly cleave

once the floods recede; rays break through the grey.

She used to call those shafts of sunlight

heaven stretching down.
        Rainbows were *Her Majesty / His Physic.*

And always when they came they made her glint.

Not Be Wrong

Any sudden sound at dawn
can throw you, like a shining,
out of sleep. Flap

and then the dream releasing
mist, a swishing wing:
    Crow

that got out of the murder,
where are you now,
and are you safe?

Who did we move to
under the slumber-sun,
what baritone …

Odd how dreams
can summon flux that
duplicates in day—

like flicker on a wall
beyond a flame, the
stain behind a veil.

I tap into the peep-hole
grey and animate
the image:

We're swaying to
the tune and orchestration.
Less mist—we'd be revealed,

wishing for things we want
to say and write each other
and not be wrong.

Our forehead-warmth
like solar
third-eye light.

Mutables

The hallway from the bedroom to the bathroom fails to link.
Light left on for safety
                    blinks ·
votives in the toilet-stall like candles in a sanctuary: fire as reminder
that the one who lit it used a match & hand.
TVs in the sitting room & bedroom are in-sync — sound
turned down to silent picture flicker.

Little brown mouse goes in and out of the wall,
                           now how about sister …

I think this is a piece of mind un-
                   moored in the ether;

        don't know why the brain won't put it back.

           Instead you come to me believing

I am steady in this skin and have the panacea.

    I am just as mutable as you —
                  tilted, turning
          at the verge,

      compulsively adjusting ~

Tone Poem

We've been living with two selves all along—
the one we're slowly getting to know
& the witnessing one: becoming.
Stunned from seeing the ugly double—

red-eyed dandy, anus-brain. Skin
sans graft, the inner walls
concussed. We're at the crux of wonderment
& tech sophistication: The candles wax

when we turn them on by converter > point & click.
Today you're mooning far away, un-
fastened at the front. Maybe a mouth sounds
mad if it rattles on of hurt & hazing.

But what a thing to be blamed for
wanting solace. I tell you sleep is hygiene
& I'm not beside the point.
Imagine walking on the spot of constant luminosity,

wherever you look, the lot beyond > dissolving.
Lead in the breastbone breaking / chaos /
process of creation /
& all the in-between degrees of grey.

Traffic

Berthed into the middle of things, it's up to us
to redirect. We of the fraught begotten bodies,

pixilated thoughts, all in some way bent to be connected.
The smashed raccoon on Bloor was my cocky

second cousin, the woman in the badger mask,
my other. She owns me like a bit of breath.

Put your head to mine and let us feel less indirect.
This won't be disgraceful and we crave it. When Kafka

leapt to the river in "The Judgment," I was on the bridge.
He changed his name for the story, but it was him.

I was on the omnibus, passing with the traffic. I saw
the body in the water,

              sinking. Even in this minor role—
without a name or face—I feel the disappearance

              still, the deep seat
          always waiting: need
      that brings a being into reach.

May I Call You Friend

We haven't met, you've never seen me;

                                        couldn't say,

There were the days on Petřín—the grassy slope,

            we sat discussing *Fear and Trembling*, *Michael Kohlhaas*,

Sturm und Drang
                        as naturally as Mann.

            I've come too late to hear you speak, to hear you read,

                                    to see your teeth,

to walk behind you, stealthy, on an ordinary street,

but not to stalk your sentences,
                                    obsessive and possessive.

            Full of want, impalpable,

                                    & tongue-tied.

Hyoid

A clutch of shrubs & stand of trees on the

knoll on the way to the grave. The boy & girl
entrusted to us the moment we brought them in.

We get our moral feeling first from colour.

Let it not be read I haven't loved enough,
I'm trying. Coreopsis, Say what you will,

your other side is violet. This, the law of
complements that binds us like a thigh.

I stand alone, lay stones on the gravestone,
clover and a note > one can stun from nothing,

make the sun appear *impromptu*. We do this
with the word.   & if ink is insufficient,

there is speech to turn to. Birds.

A chaffinch crosses the path and turns to crow.
Black wings flapping echo in my hyoid: bone

at the base of the tongue, unlike any other:

little wish that breaks away from pre-articulation.
It's the story of the hyoid to enable complex

human speech, its deft manipulations.

You touched my horseshoe-U by stealth
and bent the lesser horns.

Calm,

not so long ago / the river ambling through the valley /

easy in the aptitude of being in the blue beside the fireweed

and pocket gophers stomping on the vandal grass / the white-tailed

deer cavorting through the forest by the Bow / You know them

by their upheld tails / the hump on the back of the bear that makes

him grizzly / He hangs his head like a mendicant in a hood pulled

close as a cowl / Close / to thwart intrusive thoughts and all

the cosmic causes / Smack of bitter wind and rage / and water

like barrage / Sky is so suffused and low now / ink

could sink from it any second //

Messenger Suite

Loon

No one's remorse is like your remorse.
Even at the start of spring,
that is to say
the start of love,
your call holds every memory of dejection.
And you think I have understood the source.

Rook

Feathers the colour of onyx,
colour of toenails —
black and bruised.
Language coarse as curse.
Blatant gaze, as if to say, *It's your turn*,
meaning mine.
                    I laugh and caw
and caw again — struggling with this other tongue.
Mine is hunkered states away.

In the garden,
on my knees, I offer you some plum.
This is how you came to jab my hand.

Goldfinch

Flitting left to left, the yellow light in twilight
gold. Soft at first,
then fulgent,
then the colour of curative music.
Song, a salve, floats over the field
and through the schoolyard fence.
The fence can't intervene.
The yellow streams, its frequency
a shift. Shadow, for a moment
trembles, making space for quiet:

motion for a confidential note.

Red Bird

I hear you,
I know
you're near.

I do not expect you
to draw nearer.
I never expected to touch your body.

It is enough to behold—

And if you have chosen
to come to this garden,

and to return,

it is because you know
I know
to keep my distance.

Heron

Are you not the tall one who raised me up?
Potent:
how you stand on the pond-rock,
your blue uniform investing authority,
even without the hat.

And none of the force that comes so often with power.

Sparrow

Your voice is back—
scratchy as thorns on glass.

Your other voice—
the one you keep for tenderness—
has gone to sleep.

Cheep, cheep.

Meaning, too little of you
to please me.

Gull

My lightness should be clear to you,
as yours is to me.
We are like enough in these bodies
to correspond.
I should know by now when you wake me up—
reeling and screaming out loud that way,

there are really two voices at work.
One that needs to cry out
and one that cries to be reached.

I'm listening. My gladness is your call,
though the hour is early
(or late),
though I never possess the food you need,
or answer.

Hummingbird

You say I'll get nothing but silence from you,
yet there you go—spinning your wings.
Is this simply how you're wired,
or is this your lullaby?

You are audible to me,
even in absence.
Absence is only a physical thing.
I remain committed—

not for the sake of any impression,
though you do impress me. Yes—
I want this word to last.
If you don't believe, let me.

Dove

A name that's come to stand for appeasement—
from the Old French word for peace.
Peace is pleasing.
Appeasement, to you,
sounds like social control.
I give you that.
Definitions are often what we want,

yet we can't force clearness,
let alone accord.
Even 'short neck' and 'stout beak'
can be matters of perception.

And even if words are measured,
gesture may give us away.

Dove is a Germanic
word that refers
to the bird's
diving flight.

Starling

Tell me: What is the difference
between infinity and eternity?
I've heard you trill these syllables—
you must have a feel for their sense.

Flock

I've seen in the northern garden:
sparrows, starlings, robins, rooks.
Once there was a junco.

Now a pair of cardinals has taken to the space.

These birds—they must be messengers.
They've come.

When We Were Fish

                         our brains were small,
our vision never forward.

Sometimes we had grief
as part of the sea

our tears would flow & never show.
Life was elementary.

Your mouth on my mouth made majesty of me
when we were fish

the matrix was our water.
Always we were washed.

Now we've air, much bigger brains,
our vision is redundant, still there's grief.

Your mouth on my mouth — unwashed.
A glimmer of that majesty.

Fate like That

Bland sand of a long light land,
the firmament split by ancient edict,
common waters lapping in the depths.

Imagine a girl, a jug on her shoulder,
meeting a man at the desert well.
Drink, my lord, she says, and lowers

her jug to give him water—
giving till the man and his camels are slaked.
Her kindness is his cue to bring out the gifts:

a nose-ring, golden bracelets and some money.
Surely this is the girl the man has come for—
to bring back as the bride for his master's son.

He asks her name and where she lives;
can he and his men and camels stay at her place?
She's modern in the way of a daughter

taught how to talk to strangers. Modern
in the way of a daughter parting with her parents'
past, entering a future based on slender indications,

faith in a distant path—there she'll meet
her match and bear him children, calculate:
evenness (her weakness), and the odds:

This one tends to this direction, that one
bends to that …
In time she'll ditch the nose-ring and the bracelets.

The shoulder that supported the jug
is stiff. Her belly, that nobody sees, is her
gleaming secret. If she'd let her hair down now,

her ears would disappear.
May I angle forward and remind you of the husband:
his trial on the altar, and the knife—a fate like that

you don't forget; his mate will always remember:
The one she reproduced with was that filial,
that willing.

Negative Space

The sky spreads out in shades of hay:
sky adept at holding everything ruinous,

      anything good.
Rockets meeting

missiles from the rooftop Tuesday night;
you called me to report you felt protected.

Only plumes of smoke, you said,
below the dome above your home. By morning

sallow
shadow on the peach and loquat ground. Sky

as smooth and mellow as a flügelhorn parade.
If one word only remained, it would have to be *space*.

From reverie of inner worlds to after
Afterlife—where everything is given to conjecture—

Put your proofs on this.
There's autumn in the aftertaste

of plums. And in the troughs and companies of colour
in this picture. The image

shifts by time of light: at dusk
a tree in negative space; at dawn

its limbs are facets and the company of colour
broken up. Yet tree still—archetypal tree—

the brain retains this shape.
I can't locate, in the files of my mind,

the archetype of you.

Stacked Cast

Envoy

I came to the place across from the graves
and parked at the chain-link fence, stepped into the afternoon —
still moist from early morning rain, a sea
of shining heads and hairless faces in the street.
All of this is folly
                        sang a passing man to no man, though
he might have been singing to me. Maybe he could see
that I'd been streaming odd symbolic dreams: lines
criss-crossing, hatching back to filament and wisp.
All of this is folly
                        rang the voice aloud and rose — above the shining
faces, fence and graves. Fusing to the cumulus and nimbus.
I listened for a coda, only heard my clunking gait —
taking me to where I'd leave a message for an envoy,
then shamble back to where the car was parked.

Aerophone

Rain was falling, all the streetlights haloed.
At the venue, table edges rippled. The room,
though small, went on and on,
we moved from side to side and face to face without embracing.
The concertina music was outlandish. How else
would we have ventured all those lunges, leaps and lifts?
I think we were insuperable and sailing over tables,
ferried by that free-reed aerophone —
the music, as I mentioned, was fantastic.

Simple Cyan

Sky cracked blue by heat and freeness,
visit rather than business. One could wash a thought in water,
smooth a stone on rock. Tune to nigh and simple cyan,
just a little resistance. The Sea Wall helps, and walking along it,
resting on a shady slope — grass: green water and lignin.
The bay-scape as imagined in a mythopoeic vision:
seagulls, those immortal horses, reeling to the heights.

Wrack Zone

This one of a languid blackness, pool-blue irises shaded grey.
This one of the garden—in the summer—wears hibiscus lips

& parts them tacitly to smile, to tranquilize the bluish eyes,
or at least to try. A hundred stubborn battles being brokered

in the wings. By the time the rains arrive, the blooms have all
conceded. The coming of the rain converges oddly with a song:

the double-reeded low tones of an oboe, or a shawm.
After that it isn't odd to see two bodies on the water, long

and lying flat as rafts, then bobbing in the rushes by the bank.
We're never quite ourselves in visions: this one of a single

cygnet, bleeding from its bill. You couldn't have got that colour
for money or love. But out of the churning rivers, in rills

of dirt-disturbed earth. Deep in the sole, contemplative heart,
in fires of the fount. And, if you conceive it, through the eye

of a swan-white plover—foraging for edibles in the wrack
zone; one of the black-crowned shorebirds slinging stones.

The day we took the old tank out
and put the new one in,

I was thinking I'd probably be more stroked
if my name were Silken. Never was I that smooth,

the fish is vanished in the tank.
You with your net and rubber gloves—transferring

the African cichlids from the old tank to the holding bin—
thought the big one must have jumped,

but where did the smooth
blue body fall? Call it sense for survival, if you like,

I call it cunning: I like the femininity of that word,
its verbal noun-ness.

After some kerfuffle, we discover the missing fish—
under an inch of sloppy water, lying on its broad-side in the gravel,

playing dead. I watch you net him—still at first,
then flapping madly, unprepared for air & crossing waters.

This fish who takes from your fingers: krill.
This fish who makes you move ... Is it

the verb that does the big work? as some poets hold ...
You siphon the water from tank to bin, wash the lava rock,

the river stones. We haul the leaky tank outside:
separate as tines of a fork, yet joined. Set the new tank up in place,

feel its heft in our wrists and shins. Put the rocks and water
back and at the end, the fish. I'm thinking

off and on about the work of the verb, of noun-ness,
and if my name were Silken, would I want to be more stroked …

Ovarian

What do I remember of that cardinal time of life.
What some might call zodiacal: Aries, Cancer

in the balance, wanting on and on
to go ...   maybe, as they say, till a hundred and twenty—

The children still so young, the fluff of their favourite
flannel pyjamas in our nostrils, in our bed. I read somewhere

that inner organs glow—deep-pink and jiggly.
All except the ovaries—they're dull and grey

and pitted by release of every egg. The older the woman,
the duller and greyer the organs. But it was spring and I was

also young.
Was it that we heard a quack and found a mother duck

inside the shrub beside our driveway,
sitting on her eggs so far removed from any water—

the three of us recoiled;
she left the nest. That's what I remember from the time

before the tests. And lying in the corridor on operation day;
patients in the hall on gurneys, all of us lined up.

I remember saying that I think it's just the start.
You were standing by my side—gripping the crook of my arm

till they came to take me. You'll be in the waiting room, I said,
that windowless cube, joking just a little for reprieve.

Your being there will make me right, is what I didn't say—
like when you blow the candles on a cake and make a wish.

After Badiou

A poem can tap a truth by juxtaposition.

Truth is often tortuous, the poem both vets

and contests this. The tortuous retains, amid

its mystery, wounded beauty. Hurt will not be

ciphered for adornment.   There's something

that the poem propounds in keeping to itself.

(A nugget that the telling won't corrupt.)

Someone tossed a pair of sneakers

onto the telephone wire. They're dangling in the

winter wind, one above the other. Maybe it's the mix

of music playing in the coffeehouse;   it's sad and I'm

distracted from my reading. The wind dies down and then

picks up. The sneakers follow suit. The one below begins

to flap and nod like the head of a bobble doll. The one

above is close to the wire: almost stationary. Steady

in its accidental landing.

Playmate

Let's pretend you're me, I'm you—we
lie on our backs in the snow

and watch the cow jump over the roof.
It's really the moon, but say the roof

and say my name is Susie,
yours is Trick. You're the boy

and don't wear socks,
I wear the boots and tutu.

Our arms are wands, our legs
are wheels, they roll our words in circles.

Circles are the sun. *My sunshine, my*
only sunshine—Hey—

you hurt me and admit it,
else your Mama doesn't love you,

else she never did. And lift me up,
'cuz you are big and you are Trick.

So you be Susie in the boots
and I am me again.

The moon is over the cow now
she can mix us chocolate milk.

We're chocolate, we are bunnies—twins.
Promise you'll never melt.

Girlfriend

Slender in a silk black dress,
your husband at your back,
fastening the clasp. You hold your light hair up

to help him see. The three of us
are standing in your bedroom
by the door. A mise-en-scène

so intimate, I'm abashed.
I can't recall a scene like this —
standing before my husband, getting fastened,

being witnessed.
I don't like to see myself
being seen from the rear.

After the clasp is closed,
we go downstairs
and don our autumn coats.

Just as we're about to go,
you show me
a small bone china bowl —

the only
piece of art on show
in your clerical living room. I began

with a thought of a dream
I'd had, of a boy
who kissed the back of my neck —

though maybe he didn't kiss at all,
but only brushed against my nape
and fazed me into waking.

Tumbrel

Mouth of the river,
      snake & cave.
Mouth of the cauldron,

cut & skull. Mouth of the
epileptic jaw, the maw & Ma,
              the tongue—
mouth of words made imprecise
                 by time.
A bestiary
      dangles from my salivary glands,
the weapon in my belly ~ caught in the craw.

In one dim frame I'm dumping bones—the wail
on your face is ancient. Apparently, we've been here
& I've done this stuff before.

Let's not say hysterical
though the hiss is almost minty …

& paranormal isn't a word I normally choose to use, except
when it converges—

      pressing a flat-bed trolley into the breath of a metrical foot.

Junco

I know when I am true —
when I'm alone in the yard
and open. *Radiance*, I say,
and *Clear me*.
Please, I say out loud,

speaking to a vision,
then a single physical junco —
freight-grey sparrow
foraging for morsels in the snow.
The wind is stiff;
he sidles, bareback,

skipping over stone,
eye-white tail erect
in quick ascent.

He comes this once
and vanishes
        and doesn't answer,
then he does —   much later —

through ellipsis
& caesura

Lunula

Quickened / we await the baby / calculate the time to talk /

your time / my time / different cities / oceans in between /

Branches tangle

at the hedgerow / crows & sparrows come and go /

Come back /

The longest while I didn't see the crack in the kitchen window /

Simply didn't see it /

Then I did /   like Archimedes in the bath /

Last we sat together / I observed how light your fingernails /

the crescent in the nail-bed / pale as whey /

I dreamt a boy in January / perfect earthling / swaddled blue /

& thought of C.D. Wright who passed a week before the dream /

If blue weren't blue / she wrote / *how would love be love?*

And what about the moon / of fixed proximity and rhythm /

If the moon weren't Luna / how would we be?

You asked me not so long ago / if I'd seen the full blue moon /

No / I said at first /
                     & then recanted //

Swoon

This is one of the strongman days, red
rust on the rock, a voice pumped up
on sun, then rain—reliable rain—
and snow on the steady peaks.

       Swallows
swooping out of the blue
and dipping,
diving their hearts out, man oh man,

this may be a weak day ~
Raven holds the swing-vote
and you know
he's in with his beak.

I am in my black suit
also swaying sillily from the middle.
Nothing is as loveable
as the middle from the edge—

Something weighty
drops,
is falling,
something from
the inner ledge,
the sound of it
confounding
down, the

old thought-wanting
round and round
and here I go
again,

again,
O purify me.
Circumcise
this mind.

Brink

I let my mind go forage
in the tussle, at the flux,

found some stray ideas
by the brink:

idea of indications faintly
augured in the ether—clearer

than the cant dispersed as fact.
Idea of isolation in support

of solidarity. Solitude
the seed to inside out.

Sitting still on hallowed
ground, wearing linsey-

woolsey, parsing fate from
destiny & waiting.

Suffering efficiently the light.

Breath the major motion,
repetition the respite.

Being more immediate
than freeing. Freeness

as idea of the brain
obliged to change.

Morality engendered
from the depths.

Weeping Beech

The tree becomes a mirror:
I might glimpse a future form.

Its ancestry is weeping,
buds abort

before unfolding. I tell this
to the arborist; he says

it's fragile foliage,
south exposure—

that fraying and decaying
leaves are common

in the weeping beech,
especially in the heat. This

the tree I planted with my hands
in stiff suburban soil.

Tree became a mirror:

by turns a plaintive,
naked stranger /

hale and hybrid native.
The seasons turn like dioramas—

everything in place,
yet set on shades so protean,

they can't as yet
be named.

Naked Maple

Season of release, the calico cat now out on a limb, waiting

>   like a djinn

for the pair in the privet to show their feathers.

Maybe they'll be trusting enough to land,

>   I hope they won't.

That tail goes on with its jittery twitch

and I go on with my cloddish thoughts: How my lips are parted

has a lot to do with my teeth, the way the cat is waiting with its length

against my maple: the one I claimed for calm and peace of mind.

Such luxury to be this still, to be this undisputed: at home

no matter the weather or presence. Bird, squirrel, person,

cat:
What grainy mood is this that I'm out of and into ...

So Good at This

I've wished to step into the black atoms of midair,
be ambient
and present to a figure.

My shoulders twitch like lift-off
at Benétská and Na Slupi Streets—
a crow alights, indicative,
        and drops
beyond a wall.

This way lies a hospital, a pharmacy,
and recall:
that way to a room where clerks
were stripped
and flogged with rods.

Pieces filter through the trees
like feathers to a well.

Can you tell by the pen
I seek a yard and gardener in Nusle ...

A tall man sheds his hat and jacket,
gets down
dirty, déclassé—
        darker here than he was
        for a friable while.
Soil beneath his nails.

Dark man to a bird on a roof.
Draw him as he's gone—
                so good at this

he doesn't die
but consecrates in creatures; story-
line and dream: the far lands of confabulation,
literature, and illness.

Big Book

Bed as low as bowing down and covered with a quilt. On it

lies the biggest book this woman's ever opened. She

leans before it on her knees and turns the pages

slowly, taking in the psychedelic shades.

The book is buffer to the sitter

                  stationed at the wall — plaster has his back.

He watches from across the room —

                  a chasm like a cloister —

      pages turning slowly, colour pulsing from the print,
a few recurring terms …

        They enter into conversation, sheering

           now & then along

           the topics. A

    moth-like quality

        keeps the banter

    light as beams
      of dust.

Galanthus

Because of the silent snowdrops,
there's compunction: *Look at their heads.*

Cut-back trunks — because of the blade,
the rhododendron will come back tough.

The gulls — their long and level wings —
are lording it over the crows. They do this

as an enterprise in height and claim to white.
White of sails and salt and snow and February breath.

Pure pale on bird-leg stems / leaves pressed together
at the tips like palms in old devotion.

The dark and faultless toxic bulbs —
I've thought to dig them up, bring the toxin

to my tongue — *like this.*
This morning I am frivolous, illogical

and minty. The hour isn't ended, I'm contrite:
standing at this patch of small

white flowers in the cold, head
bowed to petalled bells and quiet clappers.

Dyads

All times dubious,
          all times moot.

Each to her own catastrophe.

Forget to breathe, the autonomic
system soon kicks in, even under water.

The clock: to time as the parrot to talk. What if the bird were dead
& air retained that squawking lexicon, what then?

Brother, your force was abortive. Your name supposed to be
Leif but you never arrived;

                    I see you
                    in the dyad >

The heart is first an organ of warmth—everyone born with a torch
& a personal flurry.

Sidewise

Remarkable yet ordinary—
                        glass in a wooden casement.

One I have in mind is sitting, looking inside out: the window
with its lapidary shadows.

Handy how it let itself be tapped: You can't mistake
the clarion quality glass has.

Parts of a poem kept knocking along
my thoughts

            like a cart on a slope. Spinning,
quiv'ring, veering over

                        those enfolded in feeling
are like those with no emotion at all: demolished.

Hear deeply, deftly, hear like a pigeon.
Ear serene, pinna hidden—

lobe, a little buff dove-breast poking out,
angled sidewise ...

A poet tried his life at vice, stayed
guileless as a child. Only a poet can pen like this:

heart & hand commanding contradiction.
I'm trembling before such sweetness & disruption; I touch them

with as little fondness as possible. Not to be too see-through,
too invested.

Diptych

Left Panel: The Move East

You remember the double berth;
       I remember the CN logo—C on its side
attached to N—looked like a funny 3 to me.
       You remember the shiny nights,
moon-white out the window. How it looked like brides
to you, and ghosts.
I remember long slow days, the whistle and the shunt.
Chugging from the world
we knew, into a fuggier other. You remember walking—
two young sisters—to the breakfast car.
You got stuck in the ice-car, thought I left you there
to freeze. I remember the heavy door,
the wobble between the cars, running for help
to get you out and holding you like a mother.

You remember Dad at Union Station, come
to pick us up. The crew-cut and the boots, his handsome
laugh. I remember the Smarties he brought,
I gobbled them all on the spot; you saved the blues
for later ... or were they red ...
You remember the van-ride home: the tinkle of metal,
       machine-oil smell; parts of every shape
and size, stored in trays and containers. I remember
hating the place called home, the place called
school; fainting on the sidewalk when two big girls
pulled my hair; coming to on the concrete >
four wide eyes
above my face, two raw and mocking mouths:
breath the smell of cafeteria meat.

Right Panel: The Golden Mile, The Bluffs

I first heard told of The Golden Mile at six—we were new to the city—
and lived for a while in a low-rise rental near Zion-Wexford Church.

I loved the sound of Zion and remember the church for the graves.
Once we went, Odette and I, to walk amongst the headstones. *The dead,*

my sister quipped, *are living! Look, they're pushing worms from the earth!*
My sister had an impish sense of humour. (She still does.) The graveyard

grass was pristine green, but I could swear I felt those worms against
the soles of my shoes. That was the whirl of my child-mind. And when

our mother said, one day, *We're going to The Golden Mile,* I conjured
something Disney-like, magnificent. The Queen, our mom declaimed,

had come to The Golden Mile from London > Buckingham Palace
to Scarborough West. This, I later learned, was true. Though at the time

I thought our mum was bluffing. For what would the Queen of England
want with a strip mall of retail shops. And nothing there, it turned out,

actually golden. I was much more charmed by The Bluffs. Our father
called them Cathedral Bluffs the day he brought us there to gaze

at the Lake. Odette and I, wide-eyed and quiet, stood beside our
dad in the face of the wind. The wind grew sharp and buckled

as we breathed it from the top of the cliffs—they as pale as a stand of
Queen Anne's lace. Magnificent, for real. Dad was doing well that day.

We watched him doing well and we were happy. But in the watercolour
Bluffs he painted after that, he made the great pale cliffs appear grey-black.

Sock Doll

He came at a time of hullabaloo in a box with a party pom-pom—
flecked with yellow, red & blue.

She took him from the table, brought him to her room,
even though she'd outgrown dolls & poppets.

Placed him on the pillow-slip, slipped him under cover.
Floppy body, woolly head, thin simplistic limbs.

      Of what there'd be an end to, took its time.

Winter hung on—glacial as a catatonic gaze.
The corkscrew hazel

froze & broke. Surly purple sunsets
stained the sheepskin throw-rug

carmine. She lay on the skin
to join the bloody colour,

sock doll on the counterpane,
watching in his non-ironic way: legs akimbo,

arms as she had locked them—at his neck.

      Sometime in the summer—   when blues & yellows
still were clinging thirstily to green, she got her chalk & gouache out

and made the poppet's portrait,
using her left—non-dominant—hand, timing herself to John Cage's

4'33
Later, in a finer light, she noticed sock doll winking in the scribble ~

Surfacing Behaviour

Váňovský Pond, Třešt, Czech Republic

The pond alive with them—leaping, thwacking like paddles
upon re-entry. The sound of it loud and out of the blue: You don't

expect these fish—they look like carp—to breach like humpbacks.
You don't expect this tranquil water to clap. I like the way

you call from the car, roused as much as I am by the action.
I am at the pond-side with the camera, poised to shoot the proof.

Swans are on the water also—whites and pale grey juveniles—
approaching. It's possible I've never had an accurate sense

of distance, which is to say I fear their teeth on my toes. I snap
the jumpers—fish at once so fully of-the-water / oddly not; I

capture golden bodies aloft—mid-wriggle. Gleeful in the leaping,
or at least it seems to me. Maybe it's display, a sign …

Perhaps they're on their way to whale—with imminent lungs
and blowholes. It's possible I've never had an accurate sense

of mystery, which is to say their realness is their glee. The swans,
emerging at the grass, back me to the Škoda (you haven't left).

Anyhow, we're good to go. We've seen the small Czech town
where young Franz Kafka came in summer, to visit his Uncle

Siegfried—country doctor of Třešt (at that time, Triesch). *Lay
naked by the pond*, he wrote, *rode [his] uncle's motorcycle,*

*herded cows and goats, played quoits; fell for a shortsighted
girl by way of her fat foreshortened legs, and went to temple.*

Husband

You photographed me standing with our tour guide
in Christchurch. Big, imposing man who knew someone
we knew back home. The group was there, Cathedral Square,
the sun on-high behind you, angled well for maximizing
captures. That man had put his arm around my back and he was
holding hard. The sun kept shining blithely and you called to us,
Say cheese. His force was unapparent and I didn't think to resist.
Let's take another few, you said, *Keep smiling*, and I did.
Although the wave beneath my tongue was pushing up
Hey Sweetie treats from lunchtime on the bus.
　　　　You likely don't recall those shots, so long ago and faraway;
you've taken thousands since. But what if we would look at me
and see the bile in my smile, that crooked Christchurch moment,
my compliance.

The Thought Begot

I tended the thought, the thought begot voice.
I listened to the voice divide:
They sometimes spoke transparently but mostly overcast:
the crocus and the lake—
the oh and ache;
stable floor, the open door—
inside-out, the (g)host;
ether in the weather, wet her, eat her, hear the heat.
Heart like a bird in a box, its syrinx, out of which the saying—

                                        If it rains
while the sun is shining the devil is whipping his wife for smiling.
In other words, the vanishing point is echo.

Alone, almost, in Cairo

Youths appeared before me by the Nile, Gezira Island.

Feral faces, naked legs—   fast forward moving feet.

                               I felt the wheezing heat.

I was by myself but for the tiny child inside—

girl I knew then only as the stirring in my womb.

I ran for the stairs,
                    the refuge of the bridgehead.

Light was faint

below the bridge: a force for neither them nor us.

I reached the stairs and took them two-by-two

but wasn't fleet enough.

                    One of the youths latched on to my heel
                                        & I flew ~

The pack
fell
back
and I was with the shield of evening traffic,
kneeling on the footpath of the mammoth *October 6th Bridge*.

I walked with one shoe gone to *Tahrir Square*.

Mamilla Pool

Brambles hamper
access to the ancient reservoir.
The pool—agape

and empty, dried to stone.
The impulse was to save.
The one hard lot was in the ground.

We wanted fresh pool-water,
in the months of hottest heat
we wanted mainly to be slaked;

pay attention;
pray. If praise
could fill the pool up,

it would be a reservoir again.
If praise would
            alter fate ~

We came here in the hottest heat
with water in our bottles,
sat on cool and crumbling steps

concealed from clamour in the streets,
heard echoes:
lowing family animals,

mothers cupping their hands & bathing
their babies in common waters, frogs:
these sounds drowned out

by bright green parrots shrieking
into the trees. Who knew we'd rise
to swooping birds, pursue them

out of the past of the pool. The shrill,
bombastic squawking: so unmusically
sure and true.

Ottla Kafka

Zürau, West Bohemia, 1917

The world at war,
   the village where you till

the land is still. Sister with your practical granting

hands and understanding,
    you are just this close to having wings.

I envision you over pots and in the fields

with your primitive implements; what would the simple tools

do without your movement ...

All around you animal chatter—this the natural

clamour. I want to have a glimpse into the quiet

of your mind, plain pacific face,

beneath the pictured thick and pinned-up hair.

Earringless and ringless in this *good little marriage*

to Franz. You knew what he needed and bore him up—

Ottla, most beloved.

It is fall,
it is not fall in the ranges of your heart—

large enough to hold this failing farm, a lover,

a brother. His eyes the trouble-colour;

yours opaque as the pool in the *Ring*, and shrine-like.

—I've longed to find therein some clue or truth about my life.

What More Is There to Say of Hearts

I saw the man in the dream—that Franz—
on a bench in the park
consuming fruit: 'Fletcherizing' it—
masticating it
slowly—for his health.

He rose from the bench;
this act in the past
converted the dream-scene
to red—probably through the homophone 'rose',

though maybe through the fruit
he liked to eat.
That colour
in Chotkovny Park, in
a garden of sculpted hearts—

What more is there to say of hearts
that hasn't been said already
by the Romantics
and more baroquely …

Maybe that these hearts in the park
were captured in paint by an artist I like,
that she and Franz and I have strolled
that park in Prague, though he the most,
and none of us together.
Of dreams: that they conflate and animate.
Of red: that it's the colour across from green.

Suite

Empty & bright as empire—
whole lives eager to be dreamed here,

stepped into on oak parquet,
front-lit by picture windows—

unshuttered, facing east:
regions of command & magic, never a timorous wish.

Towers craning up & up,
hanging gardens,

circular pools—

*

When you said sweet, I heard bees
& smelled the yellow nectar.

Love is loopy like that: like punching Sun,
getting drubbed, blessing the light

that blinds.

Offing

Ashamed because I'm drained,
because I've slept

because I've dreamt.

Branches at the window, scratch—itch
to alter glass, as if they can.

It was a long time before I knew the moon
is no reflective pool,

girls who circle like the moon
in bathing suits and nonchalance

get tripped
or stripped

& disappear.
These the ones I thought I loved.

I did.

And dumb delicious plums that planted
cankers down my throat,

patent leather shoes that bled my toes,
dresses, eyelid-thin, and made for nymphs & sylphs

not women.
Still I'm picking figures

out of clouds
and ruminating. Lying idle on the sofa,

gazing at the ceiling— the offing always

far away, tending to albescence:

White Rock

The part committed to rising
strove from the sofa.
Sitting on it, winter in our midst.
Harder in these cold days after solstice.

The year, my mother said,
is like the ticking —
sadly it goes on
till you have to wind it. Ah, the clock.

The ticking
slowly
tocking down.
(The clock becomes more obvious

the less it matches time.)
We bought that clock when I worked for
Dr. Volpe, my mother continued.
Such a wise and wonderful man,

I'll always remember his little tip—
Nil illegitimi carborundum—
Don't let the bastards get you down,
she laughed.

We sat in the living room
rooted to our seats.
Semiahmoo Bay
just over our shoulders

in the cold. The white rock
somewhere on the shore,
painted to keep the namesake.
It's politic to think of rocks as fixed.

The gonging of the clock
is so reverberant, my mother said.
It lingers —
without any strength, or strain.

Fallowfield

What I like about them is the immaterial part. These
feeling beings, much like us, minus the complications

that instigate art. Once as a girl gone lost with my dog
and both of us cold and hungry, I watched my pet—

Petrouchka—eat her feces as if it were beef. She licked
her pink snout sweetly and I couldn't believe my eyes;

pressed her snowy coat against my chest; we felt our
breath. After that she vanished. I wish her species-love

and never hunger. I'm riding Via Rail, my temple
pressed against the window: snowflakes fine as bridal

lace cascading past the glass, people poised on river ice
like toys in a world vitrine. A man in orange coveralls

beside an odd colossus, a dog as white as mine was
(not exactly). *The awful thing*, said Fyodor, *that beauty*

is mysterious. Belleville, Bay of Quinte country, boy
in a green and orange hoodie horsing around a room,

averting the circle—the circle is work. Tears streaming
from his burr-brown eyes, he yanks at my gammy hand.

Parents, siblings, all the beasts that agitate within.
Hammertoes and warts and boils that make us fellow

creatures. Smiths Falls in the reverie, waking up
at Fallowfield, sister on the platform, waiting,

come to pick me up. Tall and wearing winter-white,
gracile as ballet, her avian name. She hated it as a child

and has come to love it. We need these deep reversals
in the immaterial part—mutual to dog and Other and swan.

Moly

It pleasured us to bend,
      slip moveless
into mauve repose,

the respiratory
fall
of water

throbbing
beyond the wall. Rain,
the wet
refrain.

      Mad
we must have been
to hold the torch of affection forward—

      Light bent back
to pluck us
with its beam.

We'd drunk the moly
steeped in tea
and woke as weak as leaves.

Better to say naïve—not mad.
      Just charmed,
or simply artless.

Satellites

Whole in the heavens,
moon-pool, looming
       fragment
of a looking glass:

I am nothing to look at
in this dry moth-
dusty body;
why pity my dimming eyes, Albino?

Your attributes are mathematical
—magic. Even in sleep

I soak your shine / a fraction of your light.
But what you count as mercy is my blight.

I want not to be
looked back at.
It's a very delicate thing,
this winging.

Likeness

Moonglow through the bedroom blinds

& tinkling stars
or if not stars—chimes on the back verandah.

       So long have we been lying here,

our motionlessness composes—
the highest notes are ghostly,

almost godlike.   What is likeness ...

I've been asking people what the scent
of chrysanthemum is like.

Earthy, some have answered. *Piney.*

Like nothing, most reply, by which they must mean
nothing else.

Someone called it *step toward death.*

       So long have we been lying here,
our motionlessness is old—

like blood & love, the lizard brain,

the rivalries, the tribe.
Like inside jokes, demotic hopes

& something fine & primal.

       We pitch a teepee in the sheets
and huddle eye-to-eye—

looking in the dark like blinded spies.

Inkling

Long-incumbent one, you've felt the back of me, the blush,
the cool and mute refusals:
                            often hollow.

Once you put your arms around me, lifted me and shook.
                            Had you ever heard a scanter rattle?

Lay me down, a lullaby.   A spectral velvet yes ~

            If you hear clairvoyantly,
                            you'll see:

                            In sleep
                  a cosmologic music
            works its way, like inkling. The ring of it

                  reverberates in day ~

      Still it's hard to hear the subtle differences in timbre,
with all the hiss & hue

            of waking thinking.

Granville

You don't have to crawl in the desert
to come to palms,
                            just open your fists.
Knock on your breastplate, knock,
and be the hearer: troubled by what comes in
and then astonished by what comes out.

The mouth reveals so much.

We cried because it wasn't us,
then suddenly, it was—
                        after the grey ecclesiastical
rains. Your face as near and pale as day
before the sun bucked up.

The husk of it: We both wore black,
drank no coffee, talked like song
and laughed—
reading each other across the circular table.

The atmosphere in the street was nearly surreal:
wet yet dry and vividly green—with resonance
from the trees. One of them
like a tuning fork, or hips—
wide across the beam, thin limbs uplifted.

Height, to us, is something like left and right:
rightfully this close, and walking, and longing—

Sunshaft

You'll notice the gold-tipped
                         tooth of a man as he
              crosses into a shaft of sun
this side of the street and smiles
and shines like an island—

       if you're not
lamenting the key
              you left in a jacket pocket,
the wardrobe stowed in a faraway crate, the
failure faces, actual cracks,
and blood predispositions.

            —I'm suggesting
        Icarus wasn't falling as he fell,
but splashing back to birth through earth and ocean.
                The scaffold of his skin so keen,
          it pinioned myth to wing,
hubris to the beings of renewal.

Notes

Not Be Wrong: inspired by *Into the Mist*, acrylic on canvas by Women's Art Association of Canada (hereafter WAAC) studio artist Beryl Goering.

Traffic: "Autoomnibus" in the final paragraph of Franz Kafka's story "Das Urteil" / "The Judgment" has been translated "omnibus." "Verkehr," meaning traffic in the context of the story, is the final word.

May I Call You Friend: *"Sturm und Drang"* — literally turbulence and urgency — is the term for the late 18th century German literary and music movement in which extremes of emotion were given expression, in response to the restraints of Enlightenment rationalism.

Fate like That: draws on the story, told in Genesis 24:15-61, of Abraham's servant Eliezer's journey to Aram-Naharaim to take a wife (Rebecca) from among Abraham's kin for his son Isaac. In the last two stanzas, reference is made to the 'Binding of Isaac' story, Genesis 22, in which Abraham demonstrates supreme submission to God through willingness to sacrifice his beloved son; Isaac too shows submission to God, also filial obedience through willingness to be sacrificed at the hands of his father. At the ultimate moment, an angel of God calls out to Abraham to stay his hand and not harm the lad; a ram from a nearby thicket is sacrificed instead.

Stacked Cast: section three, *Simple Cyan*, was originally composed in a different form to complement a box art piece titled *Life in Vancouver* by WAAC studio artist Janet F. Potter, for the Eleventh Long Dash Group / WAAC event celebrating National Poetry Month, "Confluences: Poetry & Art," April 22, 2018.

After Badiou: It is Alain Badiou's book *The Age of the Poets* that the narrator of the poem is reading, and whose ideas inform part of the first stanza.

Lunula: *"If blue weren't blue how would love be love?"* is from the poem "Imaginary Morning Glory" by C.D. Wright, in *ShallCross* (Copper

Canyon Press, 2016:118). The original reads: "If blue / were not blue how could love be love."

Dyads and The Move East, from Diptych: first appeared in earlier renditions in *You Will Still Have Birds: a conversation in poems* with Susie Berg (limited edition Lyricalmyrical book, handmade by Luciano Iacobelli, 2015).

The Golden Mile, The Bluffs, from Diptych: written for a commission awarded by the Ontario Book Publishing Organization, first appeared in *What's Your Story 2016 Anthology*, published by the Ontario Book Publishers Organization (OBPO).

Naked Maple: written for *Cat on a Limb*, acrylic on canvas by WAAC artist Wendy Weaver for the Eleventh Long Dash Group / WAAC event celebrating National Poetry Month, Confluences: Poetry & Art," April 22, 2018.

Sock Doll: John Cage is the experimental American composer (1912-1992) whose controversial composition, 4'33, calls for musicians to sit at rest with their instruments for 4 minutes and 33 seconds. The piece thus comprises only the surrounding sounds the audience hears while the instruments are not being played.

Surfacing Behaviour: italicized words are excerpted from Franz Kafka's letter of mid-August, 1907 to Max Brod, *Letters to Friends, Family, and Editors*, Schocken Books, 1977:26.

Mamilla Pool: a reservoir located in central Jerusalem, built during the Second Temple or late Roman period, and for nearly 2,000 years an important source of the city's water supply. It was operational until the British Mandate period (1920-1948). In recent decades, development has blocked the flow of water into the reservoir and it's become an ephemeral pool. Neglected and hidden from view, even many Jerusalemites are unaware of its existence. A previously unknown species of tree frog, discovered in the pool in the 1990s, is now assumed extinct. See: https://en.wikipedia.org/wiki/Mamilla Pool

Ottla Kafka: *"Ring"* in the penultimate line is short for *Ringplatz*: in this case, the village square.

What More Is There to Say of Hearts: written for *Sculpture Garden in Chotkovny Park*, gouache on black linen paper by WAAC studio artist Barbara Feith for the Eleventh Long Dash Group / WAAC event celebrating National Poetry Month, "Confluences: Poetry & Art," April 22, 2018.

White Rock: for my mother.

Fallowfield: for my sister, whose name is the same as that of the white swan in the ballet *Swan Lake.* "Fyodor" in the poem is Dostoevsky. The line *"The awful thing ... that beauty is mysterious"* is from *The Brothers Karamazov*, Book One, Chapter 3.

Satellites: written for *One-Seventh*, hand-woven wool tapestry by WAAC studio artist Carolyn Jongeward for the Eleventh Long Dash Group / WAAC event celebrating National Poetry Month, "Confluences: Poetry & Art," April 22, 2018.

Sunshaft: written for *Strata*, acrylic on canvas by WAAC studio artist Marjorie Moeser for the Sixth Long Dash Group / WAAC event celebrating National Poetry Month, "A Spring Celebration of Art and Poetry," April 17, 2013.

Acknowledgements

Thanks to the publishers and editors of the following publications in which poems in this collection first appeared, some in different renditions:

Acta Victoriana: Traffic, So Good at This
Adelaide Literary Magazine: May I Call You Friend; Calm; Alone, almost, in Cairo;
What More Is There to Say of Hearts; Moly
Another Dysfunctional Cancer Poem Anthology: Ovarian
Big Pond Rumours: Junco; Naked Maple; Likeness
Big Smoke Poetry: Fallowfield
The Dalhousie Review: The Thought Begot
The Envoy: Sidewise
EVENT Magazine: The Months of Flooding; Big Book
Ginosko Literary Journal: Mutables; Tone Poem; Tumbrel; Brink
Grain: the journal of eclectic writing: The day we took the old tank out and put the new one in; republished in the League of Canadian Poets *Poetry Pause* online; Surfacing Behaviour
Heartwood: The League of Canadian Poets Tree Anthology: Weeping Beech
Juniper – A Poetry Journal: Not Be Wrong; Lunula; Suite
Leveler Poetry: Girlfriend
Literary Review of Canada: Ottla Kafka; Sunshaft
The Maynard: Hyoid; After Badiou
Minerva Rising: Satellites
Not Very Quiet: Husband (First published March 2018, in not-very-quiet.com)
Riddle Fence: When We Were Fish; Wrack Zone
Room: Sock Doll
Taddle Creek Magazine: Swoon
Tamaracks: Canadian Poetry for the 21st Century: Messenger Suite
Typishly: Negative Space
Vallum: Mamilla Pool
What's Your Story 2016 Anthology: The Golden Mile, The Bluffs

White Wall Review: Playmate; Offing; Inkling
You Will Still Have Birds: a conversation in poems: Dyads; The Move East

Thanks to my colleagues in the Long Dash writing group: John Oughton, Mary Lou Soutar-Hynes, Sheila Stewart, Clara Blackwood, Kath MacLean, Brenda Clews, and Merle Nudelman. There's no replacement for literary comradeship.

Thanks to Susie Petersiel Berg for lending her name to "Playmate" and for being a perfect partner in *"a conversation in poems."*

Thanks to Conan Tobias of *Taddle Creek Magazine* for his longstanding support of my work and for gifting me the Mostra Nuova typeface package used for the cover title.

Thanks to the studio artists of the Woman's Art Association of Canada whose artwork inspired many poems (including five in this collection) over the course of an eleven-year collaboration: Judith Davidson-Palmer, Barbara Feith, Beryl Goering, Carolyn Jongeward, Marjorie Moeser, Mary Lou Payzant, Janet F. Potter, Gail Read, Wenda Watt, and Wendy Weaver.

Thanks to Allan Briesmaster for offering incisive comments and suggestions on an earlier version of *Swoon*, and to Sandra Barry and Heidi Greco for offering equally incisive comments and reflections on close-to-final iterations of the manuscript.

Thanks to publishers Connie McParland and Michael Mirolla, and to associate publisher and publicist Anna Van Valkenburg, for their generous dedication to the house of Guernica; to Guernica Editions founder, Antonio D'Alfonso, for admitting me to the fold in the first place and affording so many opportunities along the way; to cover and interior designer Rafael Chimicatti for his artistic sensibility and technical expertise. Thanks again to Michael Mirolla for his editorial acumen and true *menschlichkeit*.

Deep gratitude to my family, especially my husband Menachem Wolff.

About the Author

Elana Wolff is the author of six solo collections of poetry and a collection of essays on poems. She has also co-authored, with the late Malca Litovitz, a collection of rengas; co-authored a chapbook of poems with Susie Petersiel Berg; co-edited with Julie Roorda a collection of poems written to poets and the stories that inspired them; and co-translated with Menachem Wolff poems from the Hebrew by Georg Mordechai Langer. Elana's poems and creative nonfiction pieces have been published in Canada and internationally and have garnered awards. She has taught English for Academic Purposes at York University in Toronto and at The Hebrew University in Jerusalem. She currently divides her professional time between writing, editing, and designing and instructing social art courses. *Swoon* is her sixth collection of poems.

ALSO BY ELANA WOLFF

POETRY:

Birdheart

Mask

You Speak to Me in Trees, Winner of the F. G. Bressani Award; Short-
listed for the Acorn-Plantos Award for People's Poetry

Startled Night, Nominated for the ReLit Award

Helleborus & Alchémille (bilingual edition of poems selected from *Bird-
heart*, *Mask*, *You Speak to Me in Trees* and *Startled Night*; French
translation by Stéphanie Roesler), Awarded the John Glassco Prize
in Literary Translation

Everything Reminds You of Something Else

ESSAYS:

Implicate Me: Short Essays on Contemporary Poems with an introduc-
tion by Ellen S. Jaffe

CO-AUTHORED:

Slow Dancing: Creativity and Illness (Rengas and Duologue), with
Malca Litovitz

You Will Still Have Birds: a conversation in poems with Susie Petersiel
Berg

Songs and Poems of Love by Georg Mordechai Langer, translated from the
Hebrew with Menachem Wolff; a flipside book including *A Hunger
Artist & Other Stories* by Franz Kafka, translation by Thor Polson

CO-EDITED:

Poet to Poet: Poems written to poets and the stories that inspired them,
with Julie Roorda

Printed in February 2020
by Gauvin Press,
Gatineau, Québec